C000088439

A LITTLE BOOK OF  FRIENDSHIP

A LITTLE
BOOK OF

RUSKIN BOND

Navya Abbay.
Stay safe & happy.
Ruskin Bond

RAINLIGHT
RUPA

Published in RAINLIGHT
by Rupa Publications India Pvt. Ltd 2013
7/16, Ansari Road, Daryaganj
New Delhi 110002

Sales Centres:
Allahabad Bengaluru Chennai
Hyderabad Jaipur Kathmandu
Kolkata Mumbai

ISBN: 978-81-291-2494-4

Seventh impression 2019

10 9 8 7

The moral right of the author has been asserted.

Printed at Parksons Graphics Pvt. Ltd, Mumbai

Introduction

My *A Little Book of Life* was so well received that my publishers suggested that I compile another Little Book—a selection of personal reflections and quotations which could be helpful to readers in times of stress. Or even in times of contentment.

And what better theme than friendship?

My own life has been greatly influenced by friendships, old and new. Even though some may be far away, they are never far from my thoughts. Sometimes friends have become family, and sometimes, friends have made me a part of their families.

My notebooks are full of thoughts and observations on the subject of friendship— some are my own reflections, others words of wisdom passed on to us by great men and women. And as with the earlier Little Book, we have provided readers with a number of blank pages where they can put down their own thoughts or favourite quotations—or even the names and characteristics of their closest friends!

I have been writing for over sixty-five years, and I realize now that my greatest friends have been my readers. They have sustained me over the years. May they prosper and be happy!

Ruskin Bond

.8.

To have a good day,
find a
NEW
friend.

When I was eight, my
father took me by the hand
and led me up the steps of
old forts and monuments,
and told me their
stories. He was the ideal
companion, the best friend
a boy could have had at
that age. As I put together
.10. this little book of thoughts
and sayings on friendship,
I invoke his blessing...
for to live in the hearts of
those we leave behind is
never to die.

❧

·Ruskin Bond·

Fools try to make people
like them; wise men strive
to like others.

❧

    'Be slow in choosing a   .11.
friend, slower in changing.'
                     —*Benjamin Franklin*

❧

'Those friends thou hast,
and their adoption tried,
Grapple them to thy soul
with hoops of steel;
But do not dull thy palm
with entertainment
Of each new-hatch'd,
unfledged comrade.'
—*William Shakespeare*

'An honest friend is worth
more than a throne.'
—*Chinese proverb*

·Ruskin Bond·

'One friend in a lifetime
is much; two are many;
three are hardly possible.
Friendship needs a certain
parallelism of life, a
community of thought, a
rivalry of aim.'
—*Henry Adams*

'Tell me thy company, and
I'll tell thee what thou art.'
—*Cervantes*

'Friendship is born at that moment when one person says to another, "What! You too? I thought I was the only one."'
—*C.S. Lewis*

'Your task is not to seek for love, but merely to seek and find all the barriers within yourself that you have built against it.'
—*Rumi*

·Ruskin Bond·

A great book is a friend
that never lets you down.
You can return to it again
and again and the joy first
derived from it will still be
there.

'Behold, I do not give
lectures or a little charity,
when I give I give myself.'
—*Walt Whitman*

'The wise man does not lay
up treasure.
The more he gives to
others, the more he has for
his own.'
—*Lao Tzu*

'Friendship is a word the
very sight of which in print
makes the heart warm.'
—*Augustine Birrell*

·Ruskin Bond·

Notes

Mountain stream is the most
comforting of friends.
Once you have lived with it,
and come to know it,
you will find that it is always
there to listen to your thoughts
and share your SOLITUDE.

'If a man does not make new acquaintances as he advances through life, he will soon find himself left alone. A man, sir, should keep his friendship in constant repair.'

—*James Boswell*

One kind word can warm a heart for years.

·Ruskin Bond·

'Be not forgetful to
entertain strangers:
for thereby some have
entertained angels
unawares.'
—*New Testament*

'A good man finds all the
world friendly.'
—*Indian proverb*

'For there is no friend like a sister,
In calm or stormy weather,
To cheer one on the tedious way,
To fetch one if one goes astray,
To lift one if one totters down,
To strengthen whilst one stands.'

—*Christina Rossetti*

'Easy at first, the language
   of friendship
Is, as we soon discover,
Very difficult to speak
   well...
And, unless spoken often,
   soon goes rusty.
Distance and duties divide
   us,
But absence will not seem   .25.
   an evil
If it make our re-meeting
A real occasion. Come
   when you can:
Your room will be ready.'
—*W.H. Auden*

'Hail Guest! We ask not
what thou art;
If Friend, we greet thee,
hand and heart;
If Stranger, such no longer
be;
If Foe, our love shall
conquer thee.'
—*Old Welsh door verse*

.26. ❧

'Gratitude preserves old
friendship and begets new.'
—*Scottish proverb*

❧

'Kind hearts are more than coronets,
And simple faith than Norman blood.'
—*Lord Alfred Tennyson*

'The sins of the warm-hearted should be judged on a different scale from those of the cold-blooded.'
—*Dante*

'The true test of friendship is to be able to sit or walk with a friend for an hour in perfect silence without wearying of one another's company.'
—*Dinah Maria Craik*

'Children need love, especially when they do not deserve it.'
—*Harold Hulbert*

·Ruskin Bond·

Notes

_____

_____

_____

_____

_____

_____

_____

_____

_____

_____

_____

_____

_____

_____

_____

_____

'THERE IS NO GREATER
DESERT OR
WILDERNESS THAN
TO BE WITHOUT

TRUE

FRIENDS.'

—Francis Bacon

'No man who knows what friendship is ever gave up a friend because he turned out to be disreputable. His only reason for giving up a friend is that he has ceased to care for him; and, when that happens, he should reproach himself for this mortal poverty of affection; not the friend for having proved unworthy.'

—*A. Clutton Brock*

❧

'I make a pact with you,
Walt Whitman—
I have detested you long
enough.
I came to you as a grown child
Who has had a pig-headed
father;
I am old enough now to
make friends.
It was you that broke the
new wood,
Now is a time for carving.
We have one sap and one
root—
Let there be commerce
between us.'
—*Ezra Pound*

To a Squirrel

'Come play with me;
Why should you run
Through the shaking tree
As though I'd a gun
To strike you dead?
When all I would do
Is to scratch your head
And let you go.'
—W.B. Yeats

.36.

·Ruskin Bond·

People come to tell me of
your faults, dear friend.
They go over them, again
and again, and I nod and
listen patiently, for I have
known them all too well. I
cannot expect these
well-wishers to see that
your faults have made me
love you more.   .37.

The nice thing about old
photographs is that we can
turn to them from time
to time, relive the past,
revive old friendships,
admire ourselves when
we were younger, shed a
sentimental tear or two,
and come back to the
.38. present with a feeling that
life isn't such a waste of
time, after all... Friends
and lovers have come and
gone, and life has been
richer because of them.
There's something to be

·Ruskin Bond·

said for photography: it
puts life into perspective!

❧

'What is a friend?
A single soul dwelling
in two bodies.'

—*Aristotle*

❧

'Let your boat of life be light, packed with only what you need—a homely home and simple pleasures, one or two friends, worth the name, someone to love and someone to love you, a cat, a dog, and a pipe or two, enough to eat and enough to wear, and a little more than enough to drink; for thirst is a dangerous thing.'

—*Jerome K. Jerome*

.40.

·Ruskin Bond·

Notes

_____

_____

_____

_____

_____

_____

_____

_____

_____

_____

_____

_____

_____

_____

_____

_____

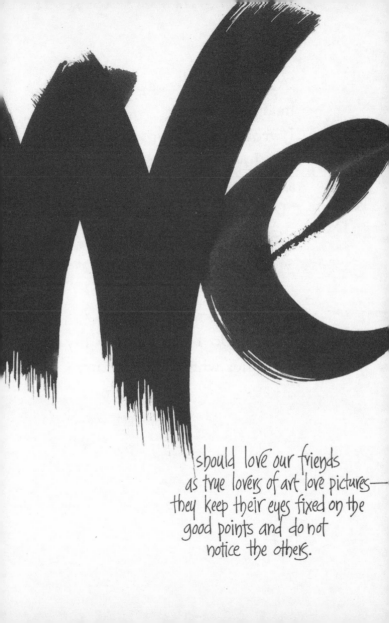

we should love our friends as true lovers of art love pictures— they keep their eyes fixed on the good points and do not notice the others.

'Across the gateway of my
heart
I wrote "No Thoroughfare",
But love came laughing by,
and cried:
"I enter everywhere."'
—*Herbert Shipman*

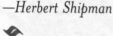

'Do I not destroy my
enemies when I make them
my friends?'
—*Abraham Lincoln*

·Ruskin Bond·

'God grows weary of great
kingdoms, but never of
little flowers.'
—*Rabindranath Tagore*

'When the character of a
man is not clear to you,
look at his friends.'
—*Japanese proverb*

'As I write these last words, my thoughts return to you who were my comrades, the stubborn and indomitable peasants of Nepal. Once more I hear the laughter with which you greeted every hardship. Once more I see you in your bivouacs or about your fires, on forced march or in the trenches now scorched by a pitiless and burning sun. Uncomplaining you endure hunger and thirst and wounds, and at the

.48.

·Ruskin Bond·

last your unwavering lines
disappear into the smoke
and wrath of battle. Bravest
of the brave, most generous
of the generous, never had
a country more faithful
friends than you.'
—*Sir Ralph Turner on the*
Gurkha soldiers

'Old Derbyshire farmer,
to a friend disappointed at
not hearing a tame magpie
talk: "No, he don't say
much, I'll grant you that,
but he's a great one for
thinking!"'
—The Countryman

.50.

No words heal better than
the silent company of a
friend.

'Fondle them the first five
years;
Beat them the succeeding
ten:
On their cheeks when
down appears,
Treat your sons as friend
and men.'
—Tales of the Sarai

.51.

'Who for any fault whatever
Fosters his own body less?
Once a friend, a friend's
forever,
Howsoever he transgress.'
—*The Panchatantra*

'If I had to choose between
betraying my country and
betraying my friend, I hope
I should have the guts to
betray my country.'
—*E.M. Forster*

Notes

'Those who bring

sunshine

into the lives of others
cannot keep it from
themselves.'

—J.M. Barrie

Sometimes a grey-bearded
old warrior comes up to
me and says, 'Don't you
remember me, Bond? We
were at school together!'
So were hundreds of other
boys, and one cannot
recall each one of them.
We remember our close
.58.   friends or those with whom
we shared some memorable
experience. 'Don't you
remember?' he persists.
'We both got flogged
for going to the cinema

·Ruskin Bond·

instead of attending Sunday school!' Instantly, I recall the occasion, and recognize my old school chum, and we go off together for a meal and chat about old times. Sixty years have passed, but it isn't difficult to renew our friendship. You have to have something in common. In our case, it was the caning we'd received from the headmaster.

'Shang ya!
I want to be your friend
For ever and ever without
break or decay.
When the hills are all flat
And the rivers are all dry,
When it lightens and
thunders in winter,
When it rains and snows in
.60.   summer,
When heaven and Earth
mingle—
Not till then will I part
from you.'

—*'Oath of Friendship', China*

❧

Many years ago, dear
friend, we walked beside
a little stream in the
hills, gathering ferns. We
collected a number of
different ferns and pressed
them in a scrapbook, which
I put away in a drawer.
Yesterday, looking for
something else, I came
across the scrapbook and
opened it, to find the
ferns in perfect condition—
emblems of a friendship
that came close to
perfection.

'Spend the things you
chiefly cherish—
Wealth and life—to serve
your friends.
Both of these must
surely perish;
Let them perish for
good ends.'
—Tales of the Sarai

.62.

'Camerado, I give you
my hand!
I give you my love more
precious than money,
I give you myself before
preaching or law;
Will you give me yourself?
Will you come travel
with me?
Shall we stick by each other   .63.
as long as we live?'
—*Walt Whitman*

'One day,' said the Persian poet Saadi, 'I saw a rose bush surrounded by a tuft of grass.

"What!" I cried, "Does that vile plant dare to place itself in the company of roses?"

I was about to tear the grass away when it meekly addressed me, saying, "Spare me! I am not the rose, it is true; but from my perfume any one can know at least that I have lived with roses."'

·Ruskin Bond·

Notes

_____

_____

_____

_____

_____

_____

_____

_____

_____

_____

_____

_____

_____

_____

_____

_____

On the road to DELHI I met a hundred

BROTHERS

'A fern beside the way we
went
She plucked, and smiling,
held it up,
While from her hand the
wild, sweet scent
I drank as from a cup.'
—*John Greenleaf Whittier*

'"Everyone to his own
taste," the old woman said
when she kissed her cow.'
—*English country proverb*

'You can't stay in your
corner of the forest waiting
for others to come to you.
You have to go to them
sometimes.'
—A.A. Milne

'It requires a long time to
know any one.'
—*Cervantes*

'If you live to be a
hundred, I want to live to
be a hundred minus one
day so I never have to live
without you.'
—*A.A. Milne*

'Good friends, good books,
and a sleepy conscience:
this is the ideal life.'
—*Mark Twain*

·Ruskin Bond·

'It's the friends you can call up at 4 a.m. that matter.'
—*Marlene Dietrich*

'I would rather walk with a friend in the dark, than alone in the light.'
—*Helen Keller*

·A Little Book of Friendship·

'Friendship is the hardest thing in the world to explain. It's not something you learn in school. But if you haven't learned the meaning of friendship, you really haven't learned anything.'

—*Muhammad Ali*

'How many slams in an old screen door? Depends how loud you shut it. How many slices in a bread? Depends how thin you cut it. How much good inside a day? Depends how good you live 'em. How much love inside a friend? Depends how much you give 'em.'

—*Shel Silverstein*

'Can miles truly separate
you from friends... If you
want to be with someone
you love, aren't you already
there?'
—*Richard Bach*

'The best mirror is an old
friend.'
—*George Herbert*

Notes

_____

_____

_____

_____

_____

_____

_____

_____

_____

_____

_____

_____

_____

_____

_____

"There is a *Destiny* that makes us BROTHERS;
None goes his way alone:
All that we sent into the lives of others,
Comes back into our own."

—Edwin Markham

'The glory of friendship is not the outstretched hand, not the kindly smile, nor the joy of companionship; it is the spiritual inspiration that comes to one when you discover that someone else believes in you and is willing to trust you with a friendship.'

—*Ralph Waldo Emerson*

My friend Pitambar was
found one night dancing
in the middle of the road.
'Why are you dancing in
the road?' I asked.
'Because I am happy,'
he said.
'And why are you
so happy?'
He looked at me as if I   .83.
were a moron.
'Because I am dancing
in the road,' he said.

❧

'If thou hast a loaf of bread, sell half and buy the flowers of the narcissus; for bread nourisheth the body, but the narcissus the soul.'

—*Mohammed*

.84.

'All people live, not by reason of any care they have for themselves, but by the love for them that is in other people.'

—*Leo Tolstoy*

·Ruskin Bond·

Friendship is all about
doing things together.
It may be climbing a
mountain, fishing in a
mountain stream, cycling
along a country road,
camping in a forest
clearing or simply travelling
together and sharing the
experiences that a new
place can bring.

'Anybody can sympathize
with the sufferings of a
friend, but it requires
a very fine nature to
sympathize with a
friend's success.'
—*Oscar Wilde*

'Wishing to be friends is
quick work, but friendship
is a slow ripening fruit.'
—*Aristotle*

·Ruskin Bond·

'I don't need a friend who
changes when I change
and who nods when I nod;
my shadow does that
much better.'
—*Plutarch*

There is no law that can
replace goodwill.

'Are you upset, little friend? Have you been lying awake worrying? Well, don't worry...I'm here. The flood waters will recede, the famine will end, the sun will shine tomorrow, and I will always be here to take care of you.'

—*Charles M. Schulz*

Notes

'People are
lonely
because they
build

WALLS

instead of

BRIDGES'

—Joseph F. Newton

There's a sweet little girl
that lives down the lane,
And she's so pretty and I'm
so plain,
She's clever and smart and
all things good,
And I'm the bad boy of the
neighbourhood.
But I'd be her best friend
forever and a day
If only she'd smile and
look my way.

·Ruskin Bond·

We must love someone
If we are to justify
our presence on this earth.
We must keep loving all
our days,
someone, anyone, anywhere
outside our selves.

Happy is he whose heart
sees more clearly than
his eyes.

·A Little Book of Friendship·

Ivy: You are friendship, fellowship and fidelity. You stand for permanence. Zinnia: You bring me thoughts of absent friends.

—'The Message of the Flowers'

'Perfect affection can only endure between man and beast. Between human beings lurks always some antagonism.'

—*S.H. Kessels*

·Ruskin Bond·

'Growing apart doesn't change the fact that for a long time we grew side by side; our roots will always be tangled. I'm glad for that.'

—*Ally Condie*

'A man without a smiling face must not open a shop.'

—*Chinese proverb*

In a sense, every man and woman is an island. But life can be very lonely on our individual islands. We need to reach out, touch each other, feel the warmth of another personality, enjoy another's company, recognize a kindred spirit— find a friend! And then, you are no longer an island.

·Ruskin Bond·

'On the whole, a tree is the most sympathetic object in nature, not so awfully set as the mountains, not so fickle and treacherous as the sea, more substantial than the clouds, not so perishable as the grass and flowers—always there, steadfast and strong, with its shifting lights and shadows, soft sighing or brisk tossing, or drenched brightness, seeming to enter into every mood of its friends.'

—*Ethel Daniels Hubbard*

'Friendship is a sheltering
tree,' wrote Coleridge.
And how often we
compare friendship to
a tree—steadfast, sturdy,
comforting, ever present:
until we cut it down.

.100.

Blessed is the house upon
whose walls
the shade of an old tree
gently falls.

·Ruskin Bond·

Notes

'Age appears to be best in four things;
OLD WOOD TO BURN,
OLD WINE TO DRINK,
OLD FRIENDS TO TRUST, AND
OLD AUTHORS TO READ.'

—Francis Bacon

'False friends are common.
Yes, but where
True nature links a
friendly pair,
The blessing is as rich
as rare.'
—*The Panchatantra*

.106.

'I am fond of pigs. Dogs
look up to us. Cats look
down on us. Pigs treat us
as equals.'
—*Winston Churchill*

·Ruskin Bond·

Turn off your TV,
Shut down your computer,
Step out of your house,
Make new friends!

'Wherever you go, go with
all your heart.'

—*Confucius*

'Friend Butterfly
Oh what a butterfly with
beautiful colours!
I wish she'd come here
And be my best friend.
I'd teach her how to count
and read
And write, the way
Our teacher taught us.'

—*Rwandan children's song*

❧

'A friend is a person with
whom I may be sincere.'

—*Ralph Waldo Emerson*

❧

'Make this night loveable,
Moon, and with eye single
Looking down from up
there,
Bless me, One especial
And friends everywhere.'
—*W.H. Auden*

Some of the moving forces
of our lives are meant to
touch us briefly and go
their way.

·A Little Book of Friendship·

'The wolf will dwell with
the lamb, and the leopard
will lie down with the kid,
the calf and the young
lion will grow up together;
and a little child will lead
them.'
—*Isaiah 11:6*

'Don't you see that that
blessed conscience of yours
is nothing but other people
inside you?'
—*Luigi Pirandello*

·Ruskin Bond·

'I like trees because they seem more resigned to the way they have to live than other things do.'
—*Willa Cather*

Beyond the last inhabited place on earth, there are still friends: there are fish and birds and insects and shrubs, and the sun, the moon and stars.

·A Little Book of Friendship·

'In giving advice, seek
to help, not please your
friend.'
—*Solon*

'Your only guard against
the scourge of pomposity
is the truth-telling of a
friend.'
—*Jerry Pinto*

·Ruskin Bond·

Notes

_____

_____

_____

_____

_____

_____

_____

_____

_____

_____

_____

_____

_____

_____

_____

_____

"Don't walk behind me;
I may not lead.
Don't walk in front of me;
I may not follow.
Just walk beside me
and be my

FRIEND."

—Albert Camus

The full moon keeps coming back again and again, but who complains? It's like the visits of an old friend—always on time, and always welcome.

.118.

'I will confess and I will not deny that the chief pleasure I know is the contemplation of my fellow beings.'

—*Hilaire Belloc*

'May God be praised for
woman
That gives up all her mind,
A man may find in no man
A friendship of her kind...'
—*W.B. Yeats*

'If you meet a tiger and .119.
call him "Uncle", he will
let you pass unharmed.'

—*Tribal lore*

'Love can be blind;
friendship cannot; it
owes it to itself not to be;
and one can even go as
far as to like a friend's
shortcomings, but in order
to help him know them.'
—*André Gide*

'Some people go to priests;
others to poetry; I to my
friends.'
—*Virginia Woolf*

·Ruskin Bond·

The break of monsoon in the hot plains, the warmth of the winter sun in the hills, a colourful sunset, a good book or film, the shade of a mighty tree, birdsong, good fortune, the evening drink. These are sweet gifts of life, but sweeter when they can be shared with a friend.

'The pleasures of
friendship are exquisite,
How pleasant to go to a
friend on a visit!
I go to my friend, we walk
on the grass,
And the hours and
moments like minutes
pass.'

—*Stevie Smith*

❧

'I can see my friends laughing and talking, but I cannot hear them. I live in a world of perpetual silence. But I know from their expressions that they are happy, and that they wish to share their joy with me.'

—*Letter from a deaf friend*

Friends can be helpful,
but sometimes it is better
to go alone. Real pioneers
do not care whether or not
they are followed; they go
forward without looking
back.

Your presence is
reassuring—like a firefly in
the night.

·Ruskin Bond·

Notes

'*Only Connect!*'

—E.M. Forster

'Friendship is the inexpressible comfort of feeling safe with a person, having neither to weigh thoughts nor measure words.'
—*Mary Ann Evans (George Eliot)*

'Food for one is enough for two.'
—*Tunisian proverb*

·Ruskin Bond·

'Friendship is unnecessary, like philosophy, like art... It has no survival value; rather it is one of those things that give value to survival.'
—*C.S. Lewis*

When you find a true friend, and keep him, you make friends with yourself.

'The most I can do for my friend is simply to be his friend. I have no wealth to bestow on him. If he knows that I am happy in loving him, he will want no other reward. Is not friendship divine in this?'
—*Henry Thoreau*

'If your friend is honey, do not lick him all up.'
—*Tunisian proverb*

·Ruskin Bond·

'I was angry with my friend:
I told my wrath, my wrath
did end.
I was angry with my foe:
I told it not, my wrath did
grow.'
—*William Blake*

'A friend to all is a friend
to none.'
—*Aristotle*

'How else survive the heat
of day to journey's end?
How else if not with the
cool shade of a thought of
a friend?'
—*Nasir Kazmi*

'A friend cannot be known
in prosperity; an enemy
cannot be hidden in
adversity.'
—*Elbert Hubbard*

'Depth of friendship does
not depend on length of
acquaintance.'

—*Rabindranath Tagore*

'One measure of friendship
consists not in the number
of things friends can
discuss, but in the number
of things they need no
longer mention.'

—*Clifton Fadiman*

'Friendship consists in forgetting what one gives, and remembering what one receives.'
—*Alexandre Dumas*

'A friend without faults will never be found.'
—*Chinese proverb*

·Ruskin Bond·

Notes

_____

_____

_____

_____

_____

_____

_____

_____

_____

_____

_____

_____

_____

_____

_____

_____

'What I cannot **love**, I overlook. Is that real **friendship**?'

—Anaïs Nin

'Whatever joy there is in
this world
All comes from desiring
others to be happy,

And whatever suffering
there is in the world
All comes from desiring
only myself to be happy.'

.142.   —*Shantideva*

'Do not save your loving
speeches for your friends
till they are dead. Do
not write them on their
tombstones, speak them
rather now instead.'
—*Anna Cummins*

'You can win more friends
with your ears than you can
with your mouth.'
—*Dale Carnegie*

·A Little Book of Friendship·

'When Fate's stern hand
shall close my weeping eye,
And seal, at length, my
wand'ring spirit's doom;
Oh! may kind friendship
catch my parting sigh,
And cheer with hope the
terrors of the tomb.'
—*Mary Darby Robinson*

'There is little friendship
in the world, and least of
all between equals.'
—*Francis Bacon*

'It is said that you do not
really know friends until
you have shared misfortune
with them. An equally
good test would be to share
days of great boredom
with them. If a friendship
survives that, it is gold.'
—*Anonymous*

·A Little Book of Friendship·

'Choose one or two
companions for thy life
But be as true, as thou
wouldst have thy wife.
Though he lives joyless,
that enjoys no friend,
He, that has many, pays
for 't in the end.'
—*John Donne*

.146.

'If you and I are no
different, what do we have
to give each other? How
can we ever be friends?'
—*Christopher Isherwood*

·Ruskin Bond·

'Return to old watering
holes for more than water;
friends and dreams are
there to meet you.'
—*African proverb*

'I might give my life for a
friend, but he had better
not ask me to do up a
parcel.'
—*Logan Pearsall Smith*

'Honest good humour is the oil and wine of a merry meeting, and there is no jovial companionship equal to that where the jokes are rather small and laughter abundant.'

—*Washington Irving*

.148.

'Locker-room bum-slapping never sustained a friendship. Grow up. When a friend is all the world to you, tell him that.'

—*Terence Clout*

Notes

'The child hand raised to
reach the holding hand.
Hold the old holding
hand. Hold and be held.'
—*Samuel Beckett*

'Friendship is the finest
balm for the pangs of
despised love.'
—*Jane Austen*

'He who removes fear from your mind is the greatest friend.'

—*Indian proverb*

'As iron sharpens iron, so one man sharpens another.'

—*The Bible*

'If I had my life to live over, I would have talked less and listened more. I would have invited friends over to dinner even if the carpet was stained and the sofa faded.'

—*Erma Bombeck*

'Your closest friend is like the spouse you won't divorce. To have both is the best and most sensible adultery.'

—*Anonymous*

'Once [a cat] has given its love, what absolute fidelity and affection! It will make itself the companion of your hours of work, of loneliness, or of sadness. It will lie the whole evening on your knee, purring and happy in your company, and leaving the company of creatures of its own society to be with you.'

—*Théophile Gautier*

'[Said the Fox:] "To me, you are still nothing more than a little boy who is just like a hundred thousand other little boys. And I have no need of you. And you, on your part, have no need of me. To you I am nothing more than a fox like a hundred thousand other foxes. But if you tame me, then we shall need each other. To me, you will be unique in all the world. To you, I shall be unique in all the world..."'

—*Antoine de Saint-Exupéry*, The Little Prince

·A Little Book of Friendship·

'When to the session of
sweet silent thought
I summon up remembrance
of things past,
I sigh the lack of many a
thing I sought,
And with old woes new wail
my dear time's waste:
...
But if the while I think on
thee, dear friend,
All losses are restored and
sorrows end.'

—*William Shakespeare*

.158.

'I shot an arrow into the air,
It fell to earth, I knew not
where;
... I breathed a song into
the air,
It fell to earth, I knew not
where;
...Long, long afterward, in
an oak
I found the arrow, still
unbroke;
And the song, from
beginning to end,
I found again in the heart
of a friend.'
—*Henry W. Longfellow*

.159.

'Across the boundaries of life and death
There you stand, O friend of mine.'

—*Rabindranath Tagore*

Every other man is a piece of myself, for I am a part of mankind.

·Ruskin Bond·